BURN

Also by Andre Bagoo

Trick Vessels

Andre Bagoo

BURN

Shearsman Books

First published in the United Kingdom in 2015 by
Shearsman Books
50 Westons Hill Drive
Emersons Green
Bristol
BS16 7DF

Shearsman Books Ltd Registered Office
30–31 St. James Place, Mangotsfield, Bristol BS16 9JB
(this address not for correspondence)

http://www.shearsman.com/

ISBN 978-1-84861-415-4

Contents

T M

Stars, hide your fires

—Shakespeare, *Macbeth*

Burn

Time takes so long. I wait here, in a box that
closed itself, for your eyes to open. They are
come to rifle me, all two hundred and eighty-six
of them, brown as guinea owls. They mull me,
leave me bullet holes on smoke-white wall, spiral
sieve of my mind. I smell a pyre. I have been
on you all these desiccated centuries. Some
days I wake and cry with joy – the thought
of having no thought of you. Jet-lagged, I sleep
at wrong hours, wake in dark, out of sorts.
Like the fruit which, by burning, is now solid
forever, my walking thoughts, upturned
left as grave heads, left as seed.

After Tchaikovsky,
Romeo and Juliet Fantasy Overture

Mozart wondered if there could be such a thing
as fire that did not go out, that burned you forever
in the depths of hell. Therefore, all of his music
is built around the hope that time is finite; he tries
to see how long we can last, because we do not.

Tchaikovsky understood cholera well.
His mother died of it when he was 14.
Perhaps it was not by accident he tried
to drown in a cold Moscow river,
then died of a glass of water.
Or did he love himself to death
            inside a stranger's insides?
Inside of him a fistful of glitter
a Russian doll,   the boss tooth,
unsheathed, unsheathing.

He, the second of him, came
for night had buried the first
in waking realms of lavender and moss
soft pillows of jet flint   the unfledged part
unfinished at the time of death.

For fire to burn you forever you must live.

Ramleela

We arrive. The green field sits wide open.
 Colorful flags rise at its edges, like bunting
for Independence Day. Men and women
 come from the village, hand in hand.
The elderly carry chairs and plastic coolers,
 for this is an epic, the sea will be crossed.
We gather as though ready to pray, speaking
 softly, since grass has a way of silencing.

At the field's edge, a large paper god rises.
 Sixty-five-feet tall, he eclipses Mc Bean houses,
Stands at the edge of time. Soon it is time
 and tassa comes: the band pounding instruments
which have become limbs. How long did it take
 to form this tassa sound of cutlass meeting
heartbeats? Of hot tin, rolled on streets?

When all the deities enter the realm, they circle
 a black flag before taking the field.
Blue-skinned Shiva poses with Sita for pictures,
 chubby Hanuman flourishes a bulbous scepter,
Ravan adjusts his ten heads, since ten heads are heavy.
 The master of ceremonies tells the story as soldiers
plan strategy, aim tinsel arrows at stars.

They light the torches and burn the giant effigy.
 Get out the way, someone warns, as
The god falls like a timbered tree.
 Flames transfix us with jeopardy.
And that burning prop becomes the love inside us,
 not villains but men, as fragile as paper,
as effervescent as smoke.

Confirmed Report of a Single Lionfish Spotted at Tobago

Not in my mind, but in the sea.
Not in the sea, but in my body.
Upon my spine, through lung and heart,
your spotted sails fly out my mouth

Inland, for decades, we sea-sleep.
There is nothing poisonous here
But the rain has plans of breaking
Fragile aquarium walls.
      Awake:
the thought of you.
Your deadly intent is beauty
so rich, the water comes whole
      A ghost, a swarm
of inflamed tongue,
O all that was solid!

Not that your body
cannot endure
      Dimanche Gras' breathing water,
but you prefer dark and cold, salt
prefer to stay in one place
currents riddled with mud,
spat out by rivers:
all that you are.
      Until we are   glassed again

An Oil Painting is Made Real

I didn't realize you were missing from my wall
until I started to paint you.

A 19th century Paris street
frozen forever, in pigment and in fact,
in eternity.

I have always wanted to live inside you,
to lurk in *Midnight in Paris* (the Woody Allen
movie set in the 1930s – though I'd go to 1816).

Let me hang you up and frame you.
Inside my room your room. We build another,
a *trompe l'oeil* – imitation within imitation –
until we lose what is real.

\

I didn't realize you were real
until I started – such that you are
I cannot comprehend.

Hector, incarnate, in our room.
Paint falling off skin like light,
flesh made compliant, alight
with the wishes of burning. You
ought not to be alive,
hiding here from gas-lit streets.
Such colour that you render me alive,
my room glowing with your pigment.
Your muscles move, take a new guise.

Now you are sculpted, Endymion,
dreaming of the things that have swollen,

dreaming of the sparkling powder crushed
to feed your closed, taut lids.

Turn Achilles, I started
to paint you – until
you threatened to rent red silk,
to reveal a pain too great to fail. The same
silk clothing the same model, who travels
in rooms through the same centuries
over and, then, over – to paint you.

/

You didn't realize you were missing from my wall
until I started to paint you,
that which I wanted to achieve
that which I wanted –
Would that you render me
blue shadow of your scene!
Take a hold of me, paint and brush
me, imitation of imitation, you,
          no
facts, only interpretation.

No painting can capture
what has not been real.

The Curse of Eternal Laughter

for Vahni Capildeo

It reached the stage where if she asked me to jump off a cliff
I would.
Burnt. So burnt. My room ripped open, made a burial
ground for horses.
And hats. And boas. The neighbours laugh.
Laughter, like water. The only riddle that cannot be solved.
You cannot be solved. Like fire. A joy made aural torture.
The video on my crappy computer is stuck because there is
no memory. My
floor opens into the US Capitol. Maybe I can
stay there and
crouch among the tourists. The dark places
            planned for so long.   /   Your reflecting lake
has secret connections. We came to weeping.
            Laughter,

                                    like light. A small
bowl glowing, filled with Himalayan salt – orange
flame. A flicker. As the tiny electric tea-light
with an unstoppable battery. The faster I type, the
more music I stop. How could these heartbeats last so
long?
Laughter, like waves. Even at night, a crashing of nervous
glee.
Perhaps the ebb and flow of the Gulf of Paria inside me.
Or Salybia and the almond-tree coast.
            Salt, become my eternal pulse. Laughter, rifle me.
Explain screams I cannot explain. My neighbors.

Riddles with no solutions, they are not riddles.
Tell no one, whose eyes can bear the light.

Icarus

Always, the window watched.
For years it offered light.
Each morning it gifted a song of birds.
And then, at night, when the house was hot,
it yielded the starry dark.
Through louvers and curtains, cool,
from the bottom of an eternal well.

For years, he came and went.
He would clothe himself with orange bergamot
then leave the naked room –
his furniture more forlorn than him,
his desolate books, his embarrassed lamps.
The window offered them light.
for sun could do no harm.

The sun could do no harm.
Still, water came that day.

And moisture draped his lonely room.
And moisture swelled his books.
The window too weak to close.
The window too close; too weak.

That night he wept for books upon books.
For years, he had loved them.
He kissed their tender leaves.
He put candles out to dry the remains.
In silence, the window watched.

That night, the Sahara dust came again.

At dawn, the room was black.
No light could dispel the frozen
scent: Szechuan pepper; grapefruit, myrrh.
        He lay there unfixable, transfixed,
the curtains that danced so quietly, gone,
the last candle's wick long consumed,
        fixed in that moment of premeditation
when curtain lace knocked down a candle
when wax spilled, un-erotically, unto spine
when boiled texts became solid.
The window screamed, 'behold,
My sleeping sun!'

The jalousie's glass is sharp and blue
like accordion gills and glimmering ice,
a metronome recoiling when pushed
beyond the breaking-point.

She, of the Coco Palm Hotel,
in the Shadow of Les Pitons

Cannot get around it, a hold of it.
The sight of it meant for admiration,
for distance, not to be touched or
scaled, not a chorus but an indecipherable
opera. Pale molten notes, and hard.

What it must be like
to put a son in the ground:
she wears him on a small button
between cancerous breasts, Les Pitons,
silent like a moon, days out of order.

Cannot get around it, a hold of it.
What it must be like
now the house is gone, crushed
by landslide, a family still
in it. Such majesty we cannot leave.

How can you live with this?
Ancient voices
climbing to green tips.
They no longer inhale—
red gnashes cutting steepness.
Somewhere, the land secretes sulphur,
breathing, breathing, breathing.

Who can live among it?

Jubilee

The earth did not know where to put the bridge
and so it made storms for us.
Water, pulled like diamonds from soil;
columns of wind; cables of jet stream –
as the earth turned they linked to Africa.
We would share the spiralling Atlantic.
We were glad. For the lawn grew each year.
The scorched mountains became green.
Rivers came to life. The ponds filled.

Until we could not leave the house.
For water had shut the doors.
Water, as immaculate as mud,
rushing round corners, under beds.
Water that disappears if you stand still.

We could not leave the house.
The Carnival band passed.
At dawn they held flambeaux
and bathed in the earth.

Present Tense

I looked into sea mirrors
and saw you.
No poem came.
Look long enough and you will see
love,
a flame on a gas stove –
the wrong face flowering.

Auden in Iceland

I

Auden sits in his underwear
Eating from a tub of ice-cream.
Watching television, he knows
All too well what it means
To not want to move, to leave.

To leave this house and go
Where he has always been:
The inside of an ice cube
Un-melt core, unseen,
A cold room within a room.

Left behind by howling wind
In a body singing elegies
To what the mind foretold, yet
Fearful symmetries like these
Refuse to leave him old.

White mountains, brief sunlight,
More dark than snow itself;
Husk of silver, hulk buried –
Beneath a continent shelf,
The rescued days fade.

How he sits and sits and smokes
And lines them with wax-paper
And bears them with glasses
And means to loathe forever
Searing sweetness on his tongue.

II.

A sheet of paper crumpling on
Vodka, crevices draining into place,
Slopes of mountains torn agape.
I am in love with his face.

Desiccated cracks, diurnal longings –
Hewn, and by blades, eye a valley;
Skaters make grids of icy sweat.
This limestone, I will marry.

Not his soul or his mind
Or anything in his time
Just rain, salt, sub-surface chance.
His crystal face is mine.

III.

We come with no plan to leave
                              Who will take us home
                    Is part of the shivering ordeal
               Again and again,
                         Even as we part, dissembling,
This place, our minds, wondering
Where are we going?
                                   Who are we with?
What are we?
               When?
                         That we leave is a miracle
               There is someone like us walking the streets
                         We always leave before we can meet
     We always let smoke and crowds separate us
What makes you go to the bar instead of walking over?
What makes you think the waiter wants you?
     The corners of eyes are falling in love
                                        why don't you?
          How tired they are, the Old Masters,
                         of cold, starry flesh
                              ·   imagining us
imaging what it is like
                         What it is like to speak to another
               We are strange collaborators
               Walking upon the surface of snow
               A bare earth torched by light and wind
     Until words form in the ice like footprints, friends.

And know
I don't want merely to know you.
               Imagine the soil more frozen than this
               Imagine glaciers become black mudslides
                    Down every bar, the long day ends.

IV.

If I have no children I will adopt
my parents as my own.
In our family
the children die before their elders
who are not concerned with generations.
The parents forget their forefathers'
Names, but remember their skin colour.
They dream
of fair complexions and large houses
and yards to store old refrigerators.
They sleep on beds not meant for sharing.
They pray for a better tomorrow.
Occasionally they have dreams of death.
Their children have none.
They know nothing of pleasure.
They work to keep what they borrow
To keep those who kept them.
Until they are released
From the safety of houses,
And find the dedolent sky will not do
For tomorrow is really yesterday.
In our family
parents live inside their elders
and elders live inside their children
And no one can tear the generations apart.

V.

Auden planned it precisely:
All his life built to one moment.
He knew the afterlife could come in an instant.
And so he walked with it wherever he went.
For years.
If there was a car accident, or a plane crash, or a sniper attack
He would be ready.
If it met him in a hospital suite,
If it came in his sleep,
He trusted his subconscious to deploy it:
So well done, his body would not forget
The intricate imaginings of his cerement.
He believed one thing:
Each man must create his afterlife,
Must imagine how the light changes, the eyes dilate
And how the world could be.
And when he dies,
It unfolds eternally.

A Bulldog Upon Discovering
His Image on the Cover

The page might tear so easily.
So easily a face can rip in two.
Two legs, cricket white, might rip
sinew torn tissue. Too
golden the eyes circled by white
as white as sharp, as claws
our hero –

                  onyx eyes,
yes
Raydell   Derrell
the boys who would
who could
make chariots
for   gun-shaped   paw

Rest   upon them   pitbull
find piteous birth   allow
    white to every hue
   not purple but blue
not blood,   sardonyx
eyes not
eyes   as claws

Dogs don't see
colour   they say
such lies

visions made of tails
        their
         empire

The Dog Show

Scout's fur is so black he makes all the children frightened.
He makes adults consider what black could actually mean,
on a field of glittering green – the last of Saturday afternoon.
Grass field, rough to the touch, the gentle curve of a head
of thickening hair. They put up miniature picket fences
to mark differences between man and Rottweiler. We stay put,
afraid of ivory we only see on TV, or when we drive through
neighbourhoods just to see different kinds of windows.
We did not dare bring a dog. For this is about watching.
As the other families marshal paws, as they despatch tiny
hurricanes and white furry tornadoes. We dare not. Stay
and be compared to comparison. Why this scent of freshly
baked bread when we turn away? Why does the grass make
us wish we had a lawn? Too terrible, the golden sunlight.

After Sir Charles Bell, *Opisthotonus in a Patient Suffering from Tetanus*, 1809

His arched body ready for levitation
Leviathan spores sculpting reversals
A white rainbow of marble limbs, marvelous arch
Cast at last in veined strictures:
Two arms, islands defiant, no pot of black gold
This face from another body, a fighting
Samson grinding teeth, clenched fist on breast
Ankle elbowing nippled mattress—one side
Curled, automaton—tip toes, loins
In thrall to a secret gravity. His, this ocean
Bending planets into oblong shape
Faulted moon-struck: never more solid

Inquest as to Death

Perhaps I should start where he was free
Silver wheels, shed of leather, flaking
His   robot eyes at our feet.
Love them, like him, my kiss on flat chest
　　　Seduction an inquest as to death,
Silver, not apple white, the faultless carriage
On roads so asphalt they'd never hold.
Burning down the road, all that
　　　Slips from these plush seats
Is carnage. Perhaps touching should be free.

After Caravaggio,
Christ on the Mount of Olives

1:

Take note how wrong Caravaggio was:
'Christ on the Mount of Olives' yet
Not a single leaf. Consider, too, Peter's
Leg, reminiscent of Angelina Jolie's (it's
Well-moisturized, judging from the
Smooth spread of the light). Peter lingers
Like a czar, covering his crotch from
A smiling James (the other brother, John,
Pretends to be asleep but his wrinkling
Forehead tells us he is not) and only
Peter's pinkie finger is disturbed when
Left-handed Christ (a deliberate
Touch?) makes a cowboy gesture.
Christ's right hand is another painting.

2:

Every single leaf is there: through
Slender veins comes great blackness,
Their mathematics not understood.
When light hits it (though no light, officially,
Can) thousands of brush-strokes become:
A telegraphed message in invisible ink.
Miraculous is the light
Swallowed whole by jet metaphor
Giving human limbs fluorescence
Bodies blazed inside-out. Caravaggio's

Trapped beam outpowers the halo
Of Christ who warns, with bodies
So lit, that flesh is strong and all else
Weak. Look closely, it is day-time.

The Christmas Tree

Though naked,
I thought nothing of flesh
I saw sunlight dress my arms,
Felt sleeves wrap me.
And then the Christmas tree became me.
Red, gashed open – leaking ornaments,
He broke all the furniture inside me.
He bit the apple off my cheek.
You see, inside every Christmas tree,
Is the very first Christmas tree.
Between chapters of dark leaves
A hidden fragment, a martyrdom.
For all these years, I've thrown water at your feet,
I've swelled my body with sacrifice
For my one wish – to worship beneath you,
Falling, petrine, among
your wrappings.

Carr Street

Those were the years of fearing needles
When walls shook, like the ground, so solid
A hole in the drain leads to the other
The side of the world where Rosie is from
Wearing pink dresses and self-inflicted burns,
Walls the colour of dresses: salmon, vanilla
Purple, bruise. Those were the years when
Walls were taller than houses, yards smaller
Than houses. And one after the other they
Tumbled, though a calabash tree remains.

White Street

The *Winterreise* is the blackest thing
Where pages of music blind under the light
Too late turned to the pianist's fright
Like dreaming and forgetting what was seen.
What was seen was what was heard though blackened
What was heard was lit, felt and had been
So many then loving in one deadly voice
Twenty-four poems for as many men
A stage littered bright with ice-men's choices.
The man on the journey was young then old
Or was he old all along, never young?
My son and I will play little caribs
We will carve canoes from a piano
And sing with light the poem of fire.

Lady Young Road

Undo what has been done
And do what must be done
Around the corners bend
Let leaf mend a lost plane

Ariapita Avenue

Can you sell something for nothing?
The man intent on selling gold for nothing
For nothing is all glimmering and cut open
For nothing at all is a price, after all, and teeth
Too, would do. Peppercorns though are *en vogue*
And the levels are all exclusive. Who wants to be
Black, when you can be cocoa, steel and hole.

Roberts Street

Before they had names: the quiet
Before, the ever quickening time
Outward signs of affection spaces
Closing in on yards, bones. Before
The thunder, lightning, crumbs
Wine bars, pews. Sicilian men
Whispering to ladies, before not
Meant for slender nothing. So
Before the trees grew, meaning
Before it was reading writing, signs
Hurting, painted – and now so few.

Clifford Street

He's always a few pews ahead
Me kneeling beneath a dead lord
MY SAVIOUR.

I would not watch him then
Not even for the Eucharist
These catholic things
He tells my eyes
MY LOVER.

For years
We walked the garden
Hibiscus, double chaconia
He must never find me
MY CROWN, MY THORN.

Four years
And still I am empty
Each day begins with coffee
And then I read the papers
A MESSAGE.

At breakfast
I read him intently
Follow him as he follows the world
All these years, not one word
MY SELF.

Chacon Street

For those who walk the pavement below, the building is invisible.
Small stores are fronts for a hidden chamber, where a silver
Car, daily, is parked. Invisible are the three floors in this moss-hulk
Where the rooms are knots. Naked men sleep outside by a black
Iron gate concealing mystery, they know. They all know.
Shreds of plastic bags, cardboard, sticks – the apparatuses of their
Deception – will one day revert to the Cathedral, with its fine stone
Pillows.   And the men will all rise, walk past the mall
Nobody shops in, past: the empty lots the colour of rum and piss,
        the old
Colonial Building and Loan Society building, and the madder wall
Oozing puzzling chemistries, and say, 'This is where joy lives
On the saddest street in the world.'

Christina Gardens I

Of course I was in love with Ms Ramsay
blew kisses on the back of her blouses
gave flowers I stole from gardens
brought cupcakes and presents
to give her my daddy gave me.

Always in love with the dark lady
disappearing at the back of houses
sweet manners in garden limbs buried
the rutted lessons machetes present.
Daddy woke us and told us, watch.

Christina Gardens II

That August, we found the megamouth shark
swimming near the water's surface, reflecting

the black planet with blood red arms,
too close to its star.

That August, we found the plane,
that had disappeared at mach 20.
The sea hid things in the shore's sulcus.

How
I grabbed the hair of the dark lady who looked up
in August, from the rich sea-weed floor
and said, foaming, she was coming to kiss me.

Christina Gardens III

He woke us told us, watch.
For she was to eat his heart.
For the house next door was
burning.
For we would wake with yearning.
For days blasted by ruin.

Dry Season

I dreamt I was late for Parliament.
When I ran along the Promenade
I turned into a wave.

My favorite time of day is morning
just after dreaming.
You can be deadly still
then make strange noises:
sighs and purrs. Softly,
they are swallowed
by kiskadees.

Sleeping, I see you
dreaming
your crossed position.

The Tourist

       Far out
near the secret cliff
I could hear only water.
Raging water,
stirred by sentences.
I dip my toe into this pool
and an ocean of snow
engulfs me.
I clasp my palms in prayer
and pelicans come to eat.
I can hear millions of leaves
each different and deadly.
How I long for oxygen
now the corals have taken me.
That Sunday, she
did an ancient ritual—
at 2 o'clock before the sea
she walked to the land's edge
and prayed to it. The
sea still has it, still
him. To be brought
up by the sea is
to drown in it.

      *

       Once, in that
foreign country, I
was suddenly ill.
The crowds took me.
hands whisper, hissing

towards the mountain of salt
made by all of them, marching,
this band of the year.
Women and men wet
sweat, rain, fake
tattoos all over flesh.
Stains. Trousers cut short
feathers, beads, confetti
all mixed up with oil
and dirt and the smell of Sea
Lots. Thousands of them
march to the ebbing surface
of the Savannah, a green space
that carries all who reach it
to the other light.
        O the black cowls we wore
with their old, gold chains
and chicken wire masks!
The stage a dangerous surface
of orange and black smoke.

        Such as I am, you will be.
        Such as you are, I was.

The coffins we carried in the crowds,
they have become six coffins
in this small yard, with glitter
and doilies all over their bodies.
Three white candles bring
silence, the wind is not certain.
What to make of this?
Not a Carnival band.
To feel first that we are alive.
To live first with that knowledge.

To know what it means to bring
coffins alive—a silent treaty
along Port of Spain's yellow
streets—is to become complicit
with waking life. On the canyon
pavements, old glitter
still glows.

*

It was wrong to go
searching when
you drowned. Though
your mother, out of
desperation, threw petals
into water, mixed salts and
plant parts over fire and
did a ritual with burnt shoes.

> *You were singing*
> *a hymn to your father.*

He was the taxi-driver
in the white car, shy of company.
He would slip out whenever
there was a gathering of family.
Your mother was the river
and she flowed to the ocean.
Her mother was a tree, with
wide branches, nerves,
Lightning, water: a crown
that bridged the continents.
Now you sing in a dusty
portrait, light on the surface
of glass, paint flakes sweaty

but living, pigment flesh
swollen and hot. Now, the
wet sand gives up this body
of glass, quartz, bone, and water,
sends heavy fingers adrift.
How the tiny tributaries
made by the waves wash it,
gently move it to and fro,
turn it all manner of grey colour
make it stretch from the East
to the West. Here the sunlight
forms a liquid orb around its
edges and it feels the sea-gulls
tearing against blue sky.
Slow now, reel it in. The
night remembers day.
A lone sea-coconut rolls.
To be brought up by the sea
is to sleep in it. Wake, with
dry feet. You have found me.

Wet Season

At last I've figured it out
What it means
to enter the Dragon's Mouth.
What it means is fired on us
upon stone, means to a higher end.
Stepping up your hibiscus throat, the higher end,
red ladder to my driven dreams.
What it could mean, could
happen to us now.
At last *dou dou*
I've figured you.

Independence Square

for Mervyn Taylor

The   line I dreamt   is missing
The   line of the brick promenade
Stretching in the wrong direction
Away from   the waterfront,   sea.
This square is a crocodile   gliding
With people on its back riding
Asphalt   bleeds a twin tower
And gray bodies   next to grace.

Eastern Main Road

Do not speak of it, the wet light
Turn the world round, take his body
Into the compound, open the gates
A perpetual movie holds up coffins
Holds up beams, galvanise, concrete
Walls – there are sculptures hidden
Where we film his bloodied body
Fassbinder's white rain all the time

Wait

How could a man fit in such a space?
Bellowed legs, lungs, cellophane wings
Scratching paint off plaster, flight of loneliness.
How could a man take so long
To know? What did not fit, how could he?
See. The man – the mirror, the shell
The imaginary me, climbing into
A canvas that could not be.
Maybe when we die, the space we occupy contracts,
Maybe the universe gets smaller.

Yet Again

for Kriston Chen

Once a year, my crazy soul begins to fly.
Overhead, the band marches past,
their boots landing right next to my eye.
I wait, yet again, for this parade.
    For this parade I dream,
to rise again in the cool streets
each limb kept in line, each instrument a truth
undoing all year's heartbeats.
    Take me to your country.
Make me the independence of this land.
Down the path of fireworks,
Wile me with your hand.
Yet again, your hand.

Order of the Republic

I am as old as AIDS.
In Trinidad and Tobago,
Land of Discipline, Production,
Tolerance, I am tolerated.
I, as old as Trinidad and Tobago,
A product of that which now disciplines
Desire, despair, desire
In the fires of hope and prayer.
Pray for us, the unmade, apart from this.
I, as old as mistakes, aberration:
Proof of all God declined to plan,
The smallness of the line between animal and man
Forged from the love of liberty.
On land belonging to you
I myself am the world.

Fun

Lifting everything I've been carrying all day
One dumbbell closer to the next
Repeating prayers for transformation.
For transformation, this body is turned faceless
My spine the only constant inside me
My body as disciplined as a lung
For the sake of it.
And so this work
Works and works us
Among these treadmills I live
For permission to live again
In arms which,   no matter
How hooked up
Cannot blackout this desire
With their corporeal accomplishment.

With Boundless Faith

Trains don't run here anymore
But when they did the men wept

The women leapt into the carriages
And bodies were strewn on the land

Exquisite torture ruled us
Slaves after death, *coup de poudre*

The nation now a marriage
Of machine and art

Our bodies came alive
At their destinations

In Forest, Wild Skies

I

The sky inside you douen
At our ends, endless rest.
The time for reading is done.
You are your parent's nightmare
Falling so quietly in love
In the undiscovered country.
Love, the contraband quality
Fathers, sisters, friends say no;
Love says no to lovers who crack
Their thoughts with moonlight.
Today, open revolt attends us
Perforce our eyes grow nitid
Until ecstasy crabs our path.
Douen, a face.

II

Douen, face me. Inside you
Are a face. So quiet. Shadow me
Grave in the folds of curling wood
A soft-scented grave, chipped by sun
We bloom atonal: years after we met
Lured here to cotton tenderness.
Moloch's castle littered with us.
Now, fingers no longer try to flee
But caress the pods that contain our souls
And grow like sun-sexed branches
That no longer bother to warn the world
That the cleft of a heart is as big as a tree
That the heart of a heart is as big as time
Douen, a face inside mine.

III

Douen, lightning makes us parrots.
Emerald, blue, red and gold, plumes:
The body of the broadcast night.
We carry sacks on one shoulder.
We sleep, therefore, on only one side.
Sleepwalker in dreams about daytime
In which we miss the true trajectory.
Of wings that come at dusk, at dawn
We miss the cries each day, hear of it.
Watch and see what I do with a face
Two eyes traffic jammed, no visage.
All souls are wires in a single space.
Douen, lightning makes us mirage.

The Spiral Staircase

My dad built a spiral staircase.
He made it of steel.
He took a pole from an old fire station.
The firemen would use it to slide
into danger.
He welded steps to it.
He made rails using grills from gas stoves.
They look like the twigs of birds nests.
They make the shape of weird spines.

The staircase is the only thing that connects us now,
my father upstairs in his room praying.
As he sits among white mosquito nets and bibles,
I punch the punching bag. I work out
what I cannot work out.

I walk up the stairs,
on steps he singed for me,
to say, for the day, goodbye.

Thus

Agni never dreamt
he would die in his sleep
one night he dreamt
he turned —

Thanks

Thank you Jaime Bagoo, Vahni Capildeo, Dwayne Dubarry, Ann Marie Goodwin, Barbara Jenkins, Nicholas Laughlin, Vladimir Lucien, Mervyn Taylor, Courtenay Williams.

Grateful acknowledgement is made to the editors of the following journals in which some of these poems appeared, often in different form:

Almost Island, 'Roberts Street', 'Ariapita Avenue', 'Clifford Street', 'Chacon Street', 'Christina Gardens I', 'Christina Gardens II', 'Christina Gardens III', 'Eastern Main Road';

Blackbox Manifold, 'Jubilee', 'Dry Season', 'Wet Season', 'With Boundless Faith' (as 'Sacred Heart');

Caribbean Review of Books, 'Burn';

Cincinnati Review, 'Carr Street', 'Lady Young Road', 'White Street', 'Independence Square';

Draconian Switch, 'The Tourist';

Exit Strata, 'Confirmed Report of a Lionfish Spotted at Tobago';

Likewise Folio, 'After Tchaikovsky, *Romeo and Juliet Fantasy Overture*' (as 'Overture');

Message in a Bottle, 'Icarus', 'An Oil Painting Is Made Real';

Moko, 'Auden in Iceland';

Word Riot, 'After Caravaggio, Christ on the Mount of Olives', 'The Curse of Eternal Laughter';

The Drunken Boat, 'After Sir Charles Bell, Opisthotonus in a Patient Suffering from Tetanus, 1809'; 'Inquest as to Death'; 'A Bulldog Upon Discovering His Image On The Cover'; 'She, of the Coco Palm Hotel, in the Shadow of Les Pitons'.

Notes

The poem 'Burn' was written in response to Al Brathwaite's *The Limes Installation* at Alice Yard, Woodbrook, Trinidad, June 2014. 'Wait' was written in response to Dave Williams' dance performance, *Waiting*, at the same space, performed in 2007.

'In Forest, Wild Skies', 'Order of the Republic', 'Fun' and 'Yet Again' are from *Douen Islands*, a 2013 e-book done in collaboration with designer Kriston Chen, along with a coterie of artisans. A *douen* is a Trinidad folklore character, a child spirit that haunts the world because of premature death. See: douenislands.tumblr.com. The poems 'Dry Season', 'Wet Season' and 'With Boundless Faith' are from *Douen Islands: Sacred Heart EP*, a continuation of this collaboration, found here: sacredheartep.tumblr.com

'Inquest as to Death' was produced as part of a collaboration with the Trinidadian artist Luis Vasquez de la Roche, which was published at *The Drunken Boat* in 2013.